10 BEST Sexy Women Photo Manips
by Larry Murk

Preface

I, Larry Murk, graduated from Stanford University in 1987 with a bachelors degree in computer science. In 2000 I suffered an accident that caused a spinal cord injury leaving me a quadriplegic. Luckily I can still control my arms enough to operate a computer reasonably. I have always been interested in art and being confined to a wheelchair has led me to explore the world of digital image creation. My image editor of choice is named GIMP. GIMP is very similar to Photoshop except that it is FREE so I highly recommend everyone try it out.

Every image in this book was created by my editing a photograph. In each case I was given permission to create a video tutorial showing how I altered the photograph. Visit the ClassicsGold Youtube channel to view videos of how each painting was created. The video will supply links to the original photo, the model and the photographer (when available). The ebook version of this book has hyperlinks for easy navigation.

I hope you enjoy sharing these images as much as I enjoyed creating them.

Doll in a Box

A doll sits alone in her toy box waiting for someone to play with her.

Photographer: Alex
Model: Kitty-Honey

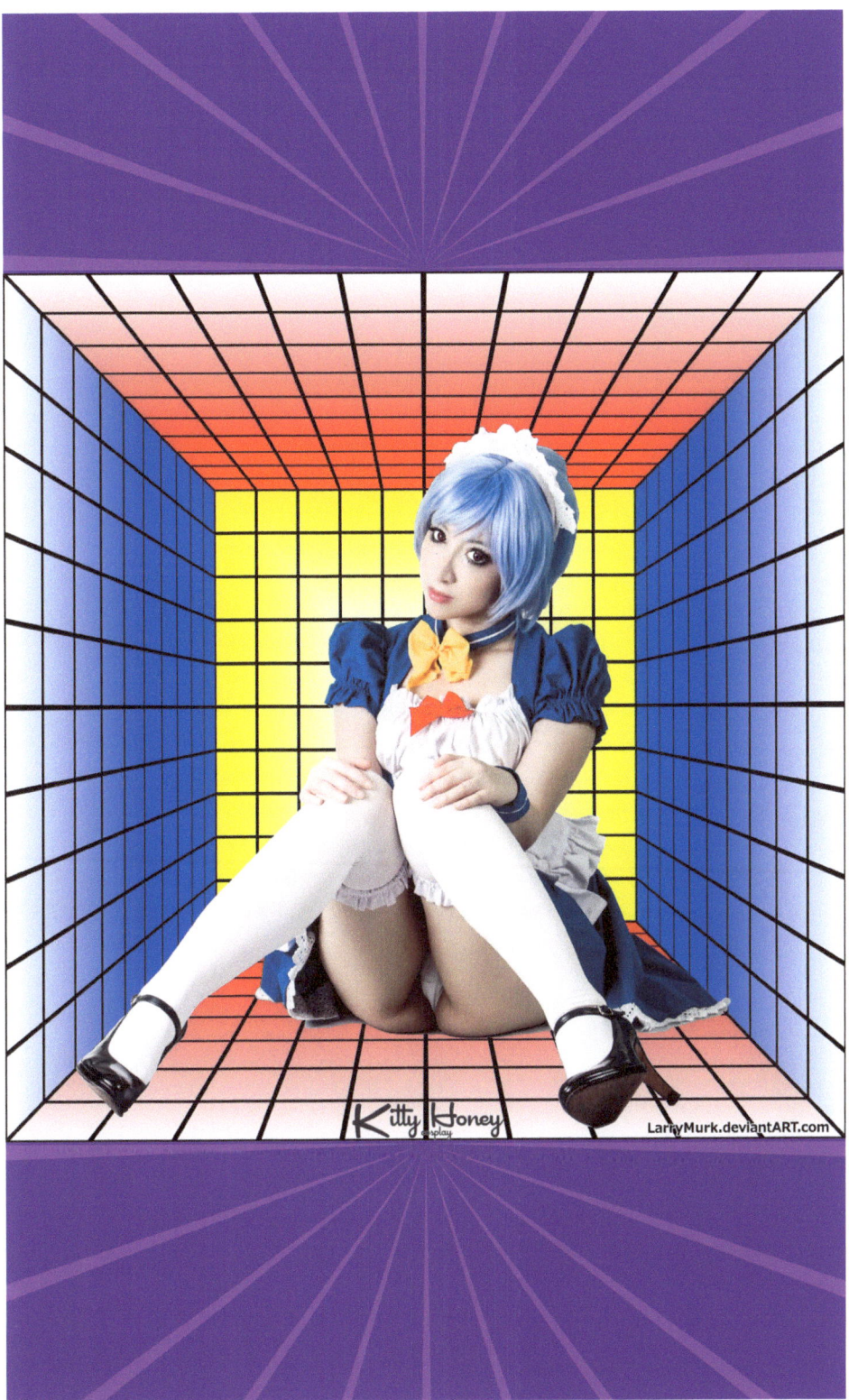

Red Lipstick

A lovely face in shades of black and white with hints of orange create the backdrop for glistening red lips.

Model: Sara

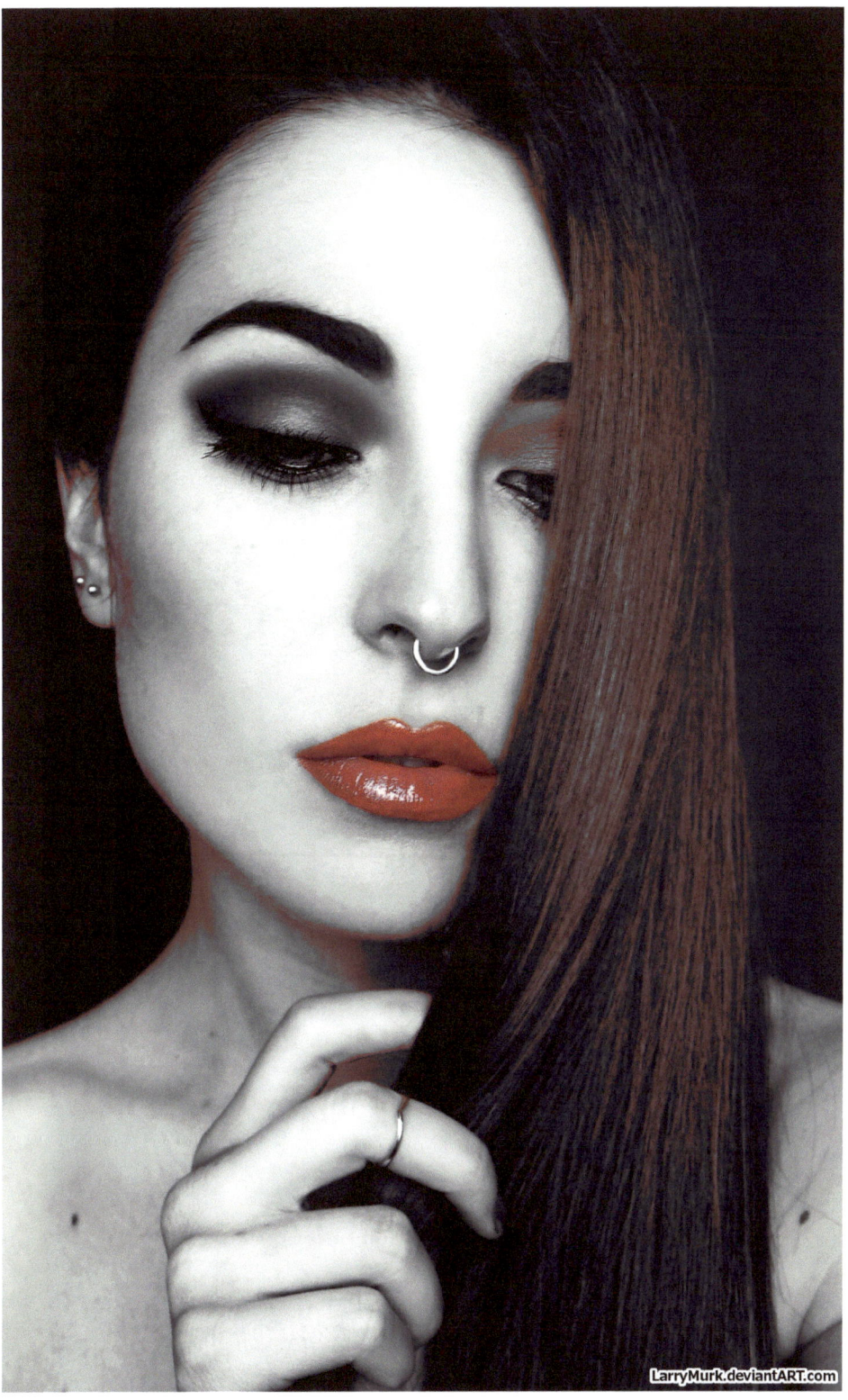

Singapore Gals

A couple of colorfully costumed cartoon gals dance their way along a dusty dirt road in Singapore.

Photographer: Nicholas Vax
Models: Eriza Aya & Amy Dakota

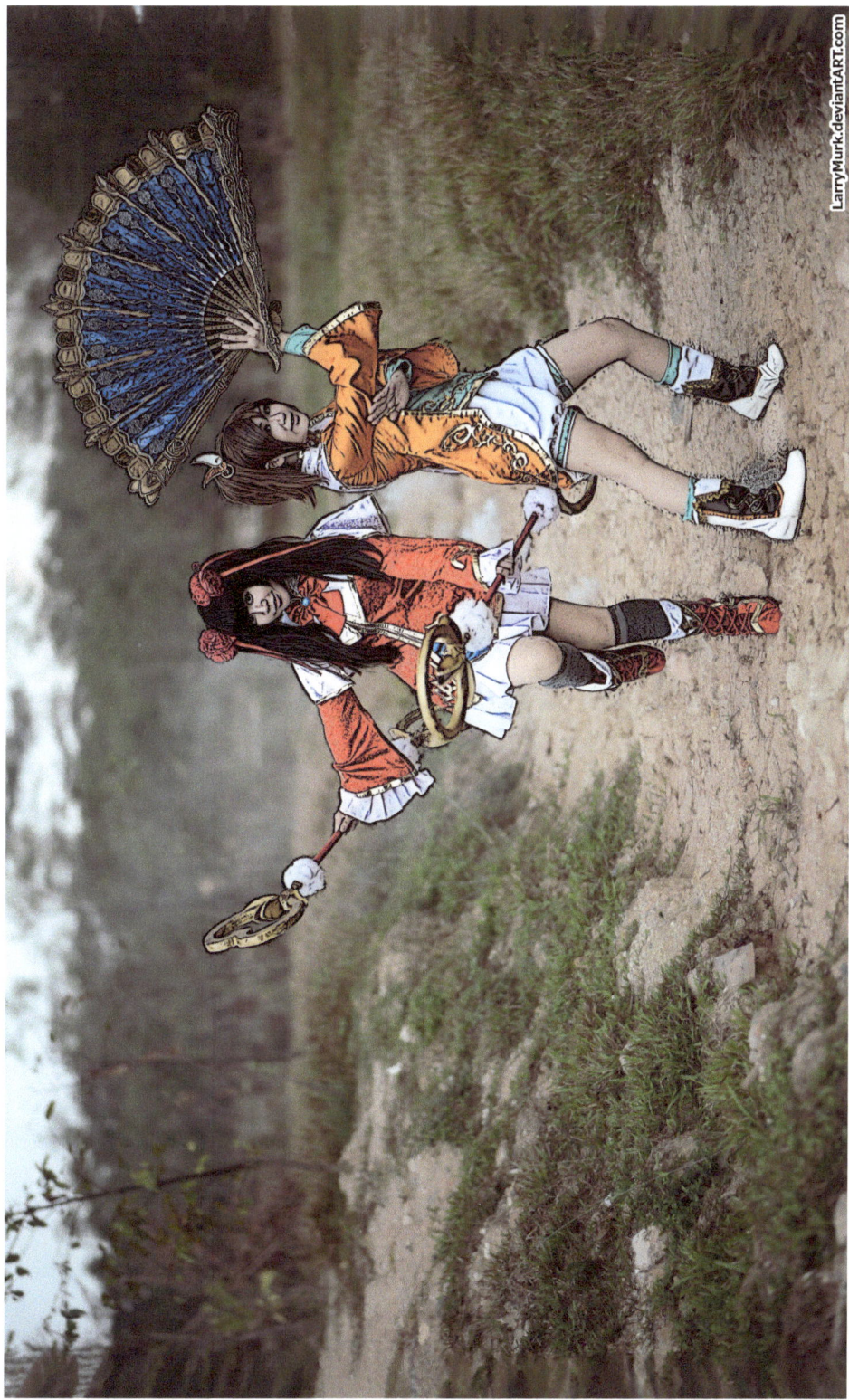

Fiery Hair

Her glowing hot silhouette etched an unforgettable image on the dark horizon with burning fiery hair emitting an inferno of swirling flames.

Photographer: Daniel West
Model: Brynn

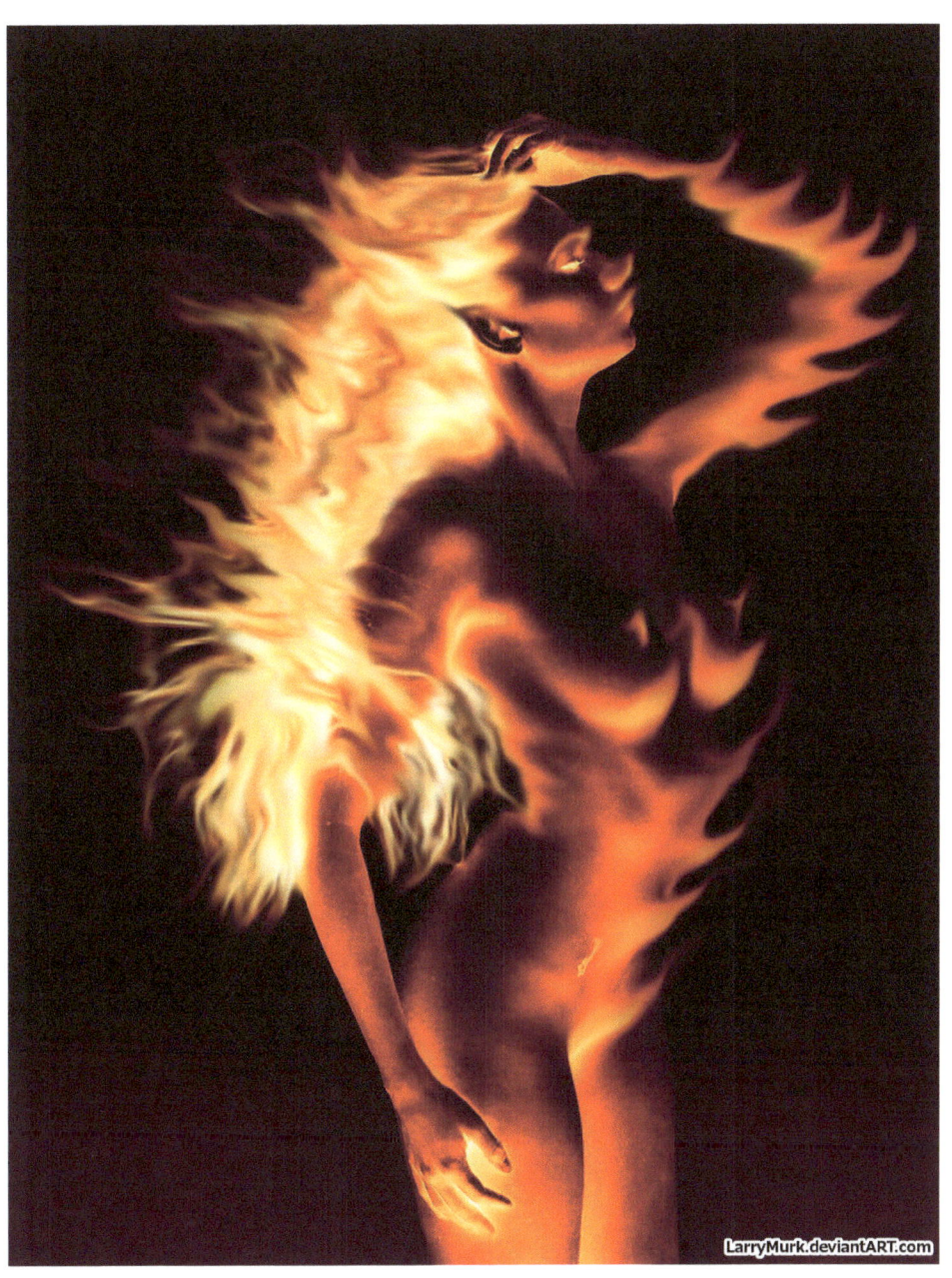

A Cube of Characters

Ivy adorns three faces of this cube costumed as Alice in Wonderland, Wonder Woman and Star Trek.

Photographer: MC Illusion
Model: Ivy

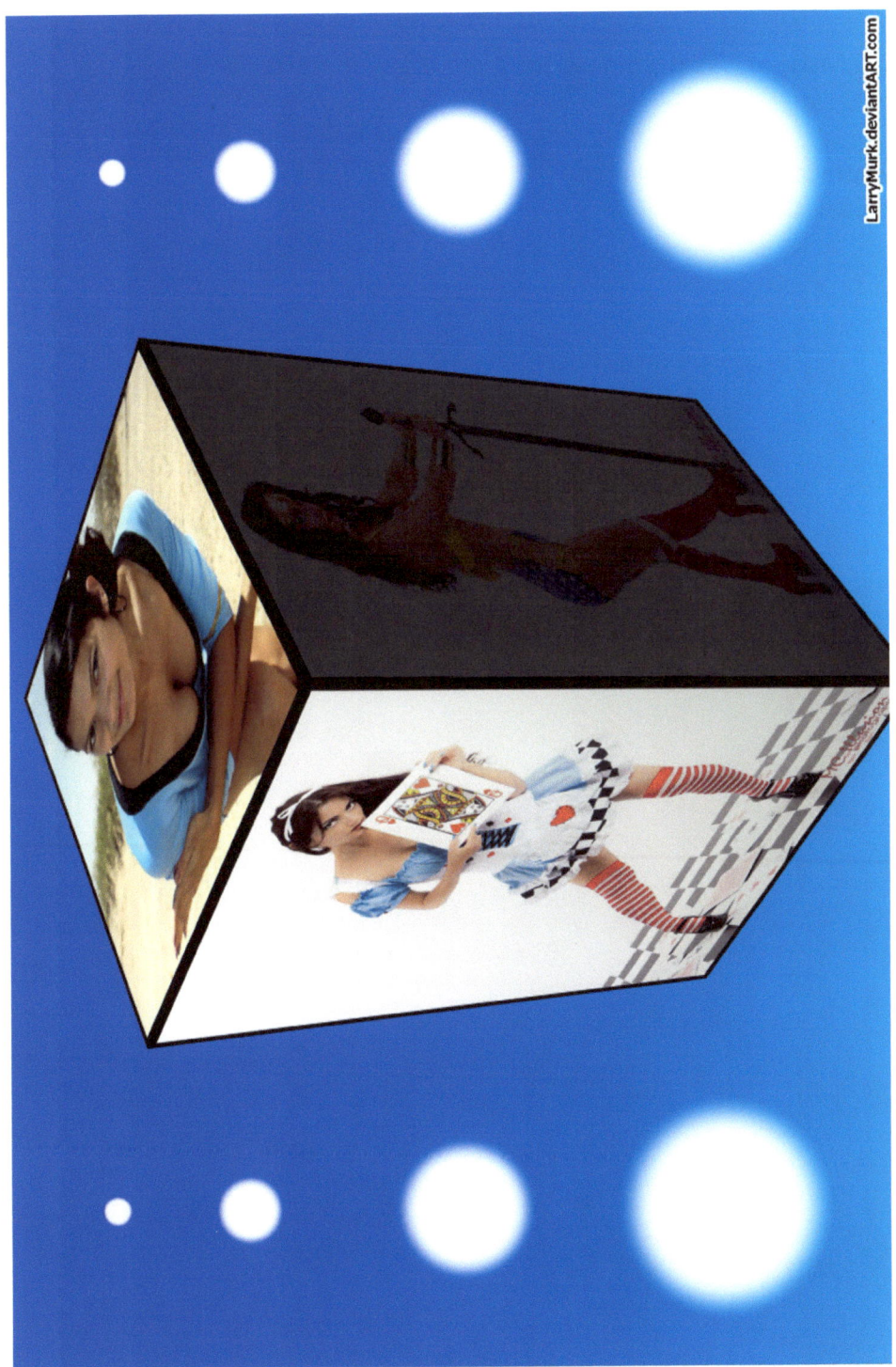

Riding a Bobcat

Chelasea enjoying a trip around town riding on her pet bobcat.

Photographer: catsuitmodel
Model: Chelasea

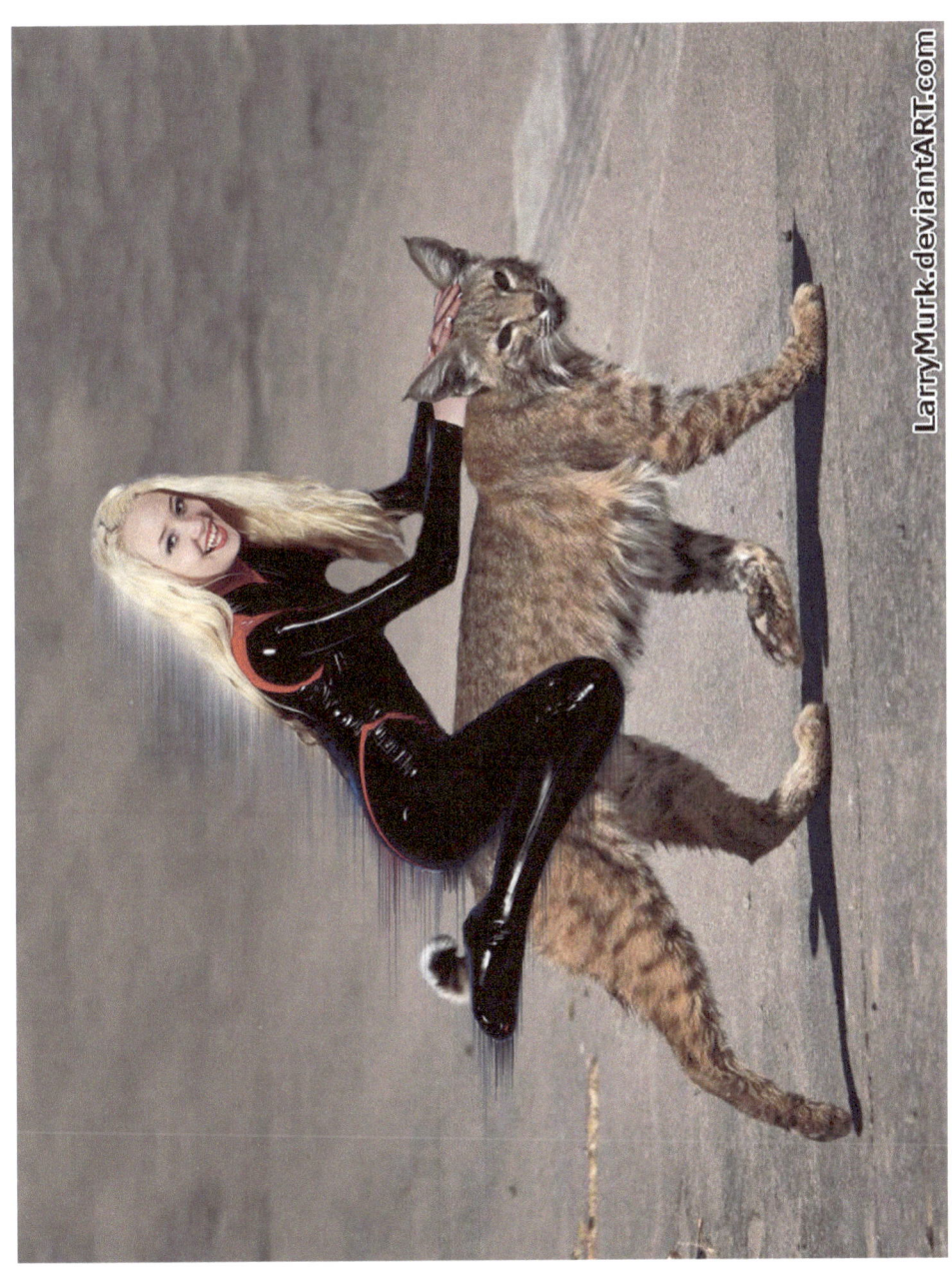

Pink Hair in Shower

A shower sprays a cone of sparkling water over her feminine curves and pink locks.

Model: Annu

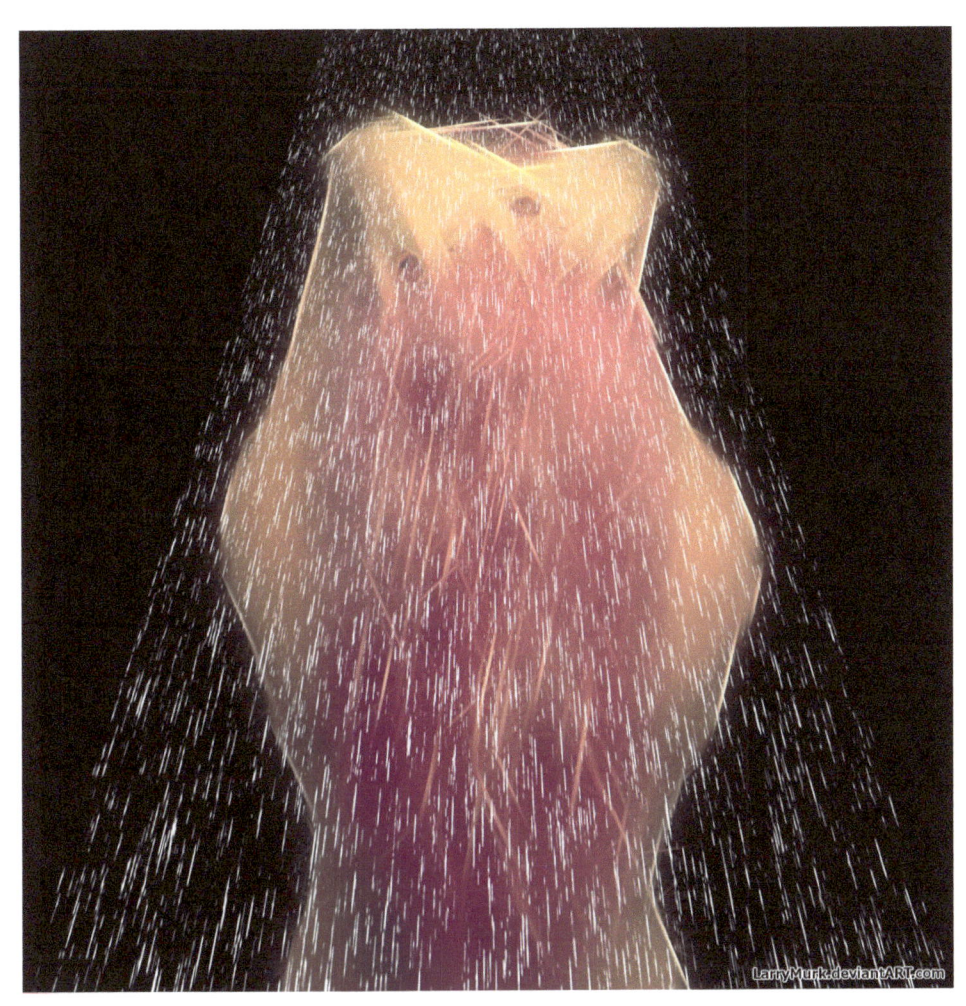

Christmas Present

Christmas is here and Kitty-Honey has dressed up in her sexy Santa outfit to give you a very special present.

Photographer: Alex
Model: Kitty-Honey

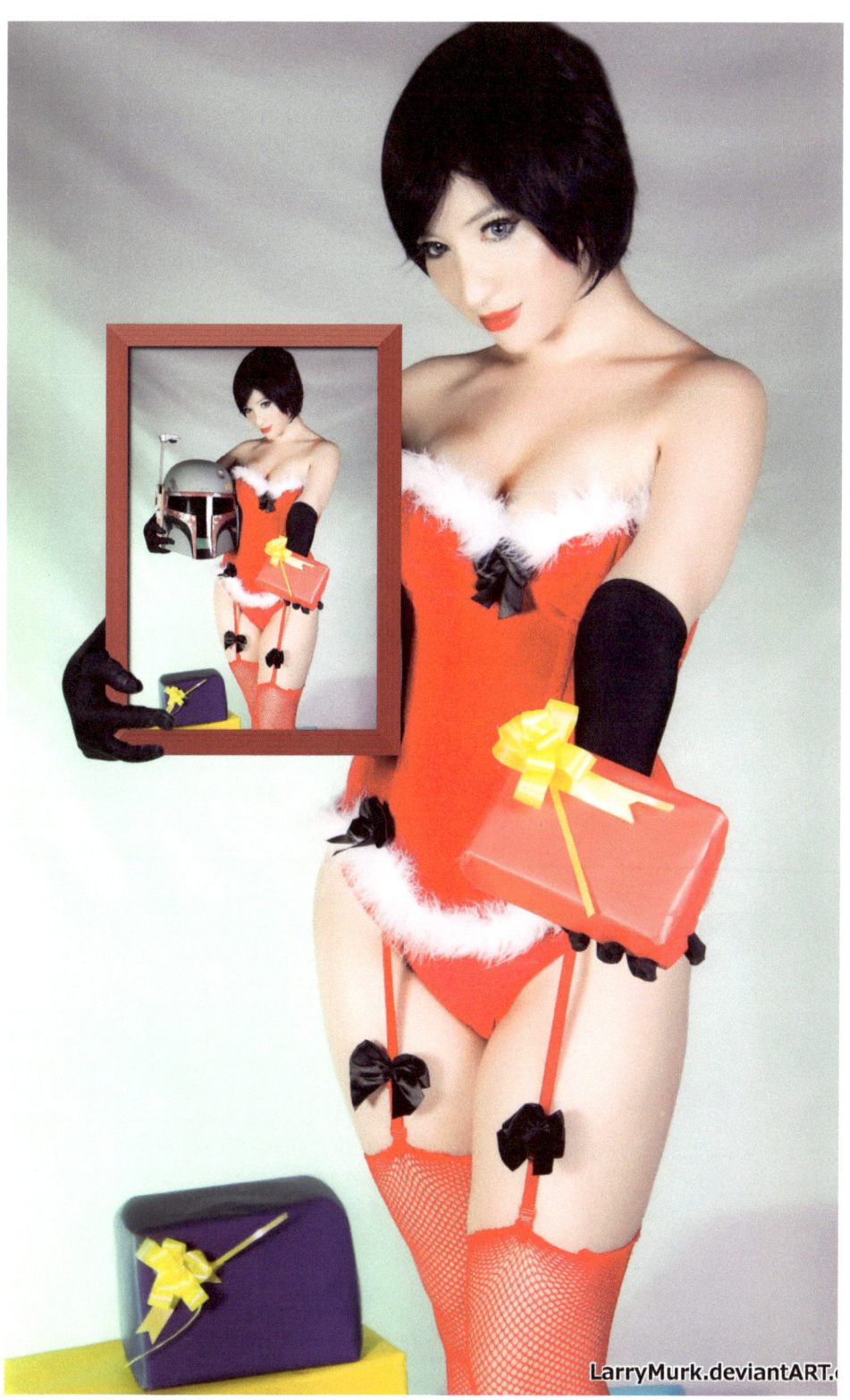

Officer in Red Heels

This officer is dressed to the nines in her Corporal in the Marines uniform and red heeled shoes.

Photographer: Matthew Murray
Model: Victoria

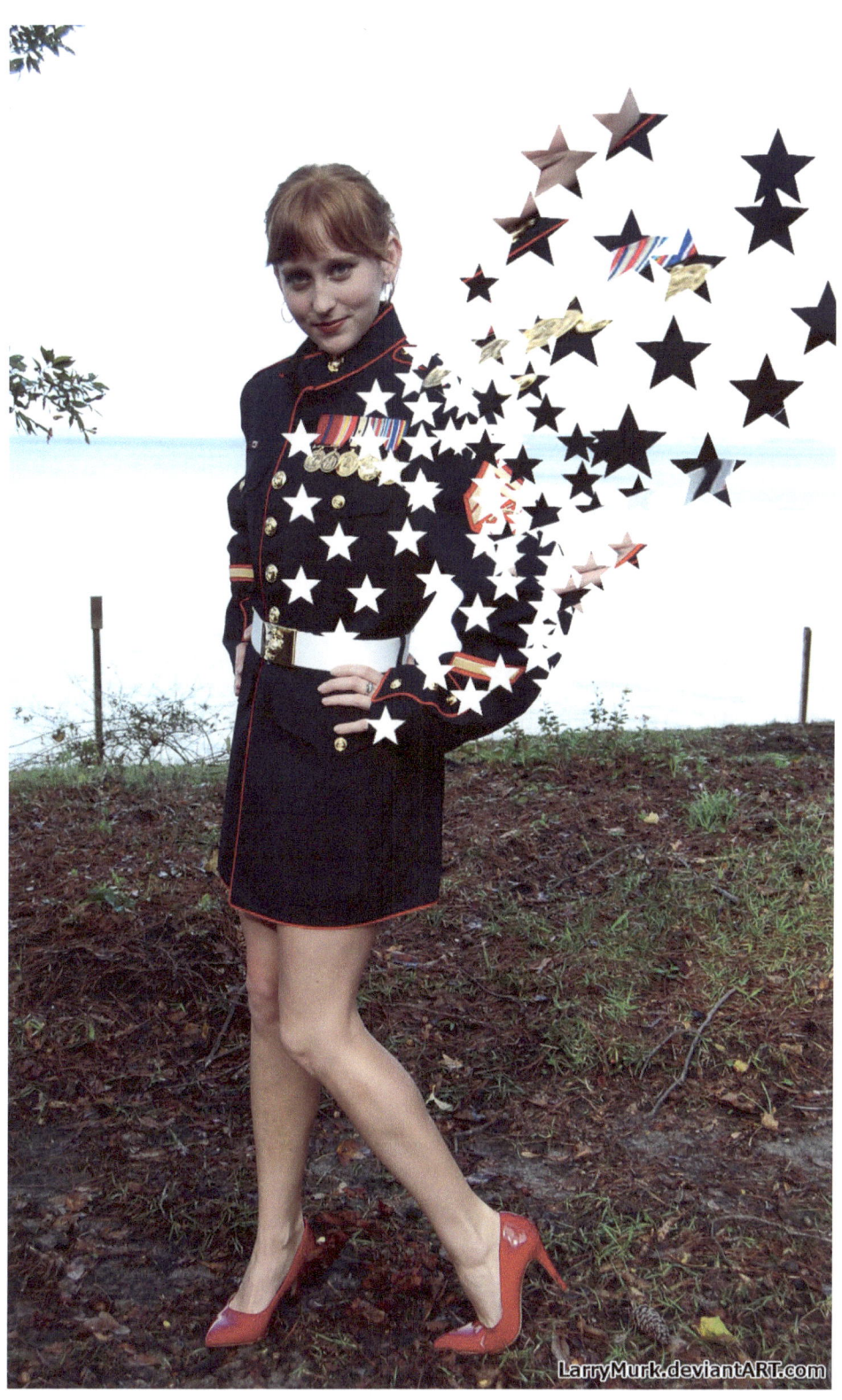

Angelic Pose

She poses still as a statue in the courtyard enrobed in a brilliant leotard outfit with angel wings looking onward to see what the future is bringing.

Model: Kou Usagi

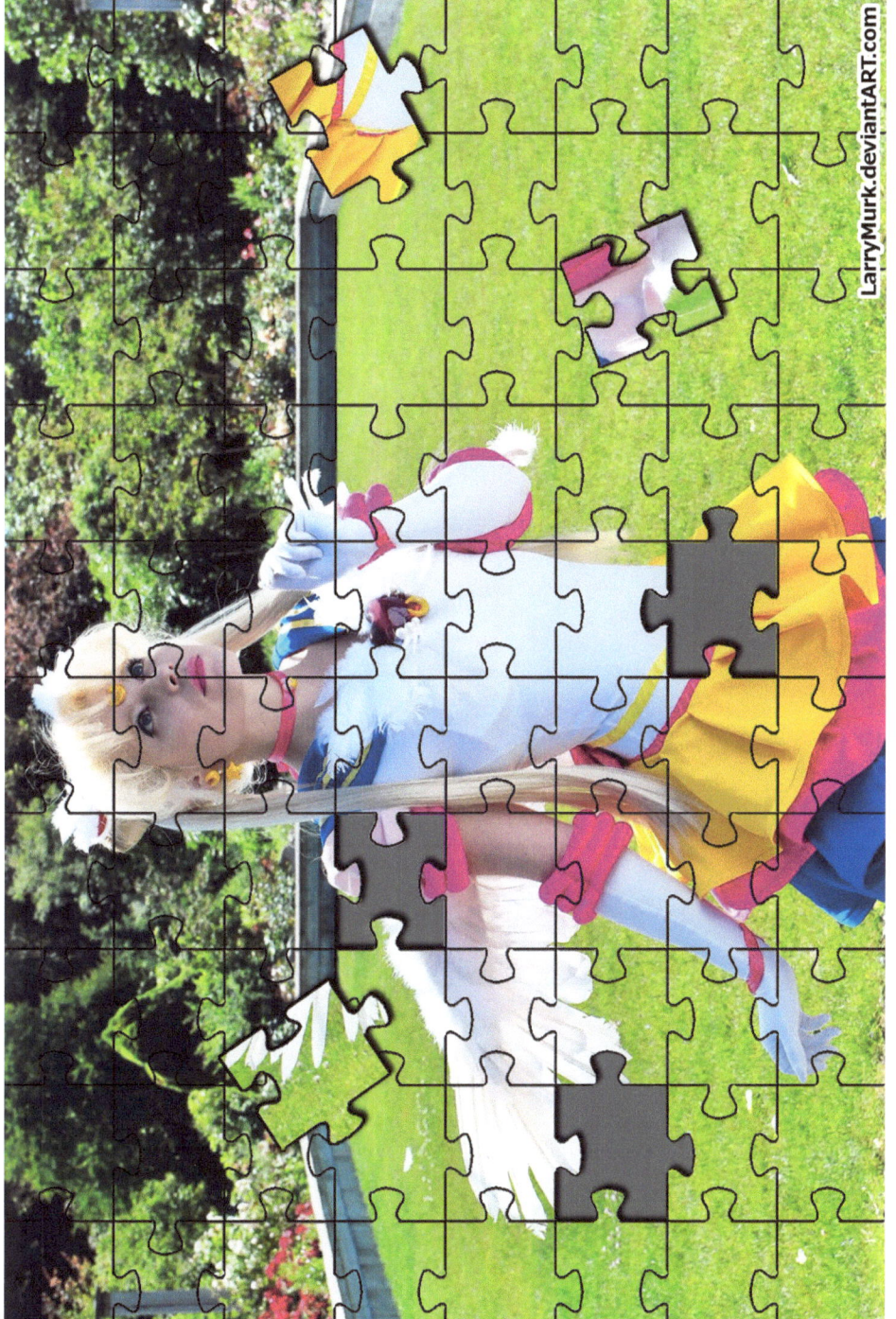

www.ingramcontent.com/pod-product-compliance
Lightning Source LLC
Chambersburg PA
CBHW041623180526
45159CB00002BC/992